W9-AGI-303

DISCARD
WITHDRAWAL

John Quincy Adams

Our PRESIDENTS

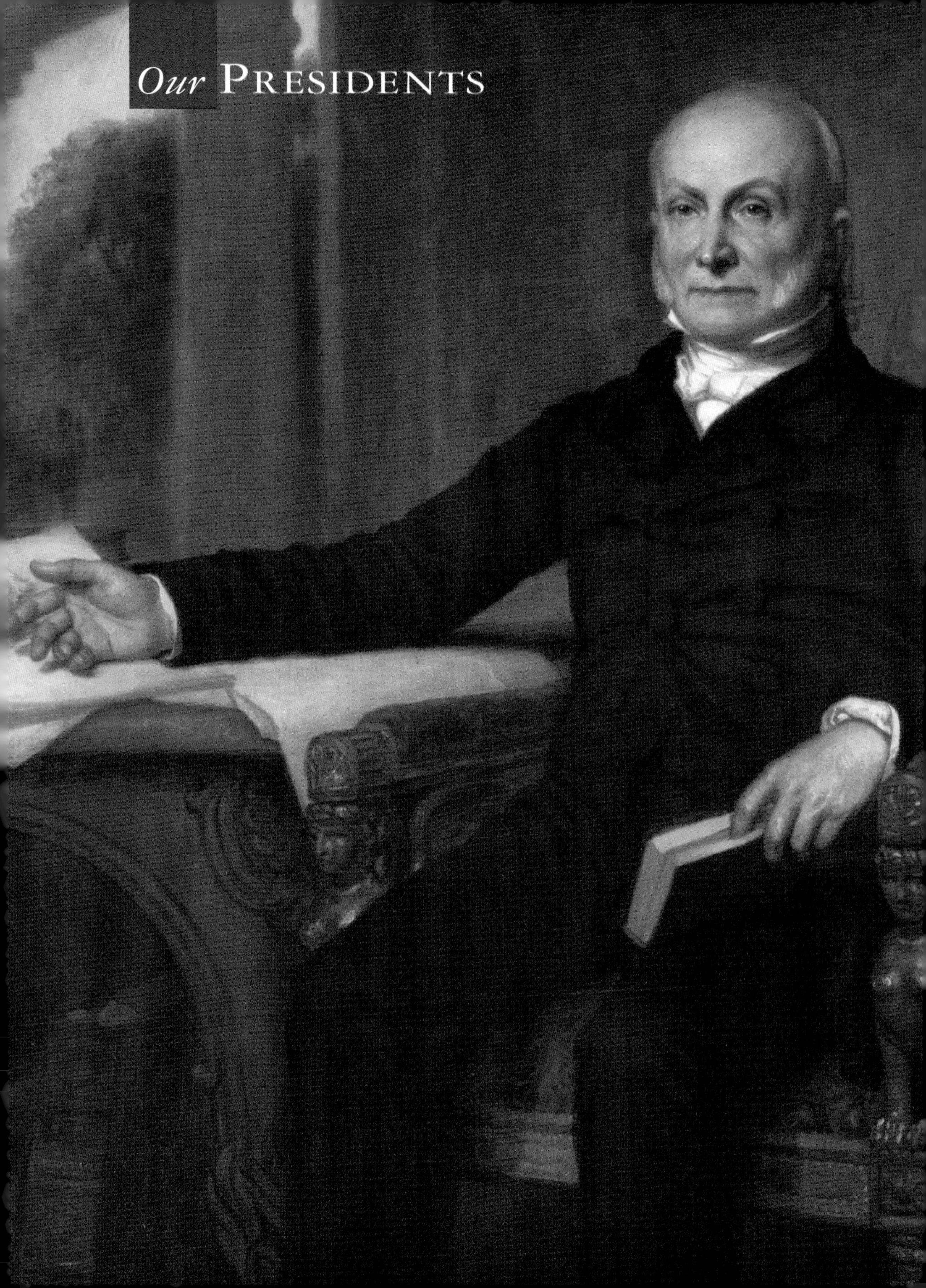

John Quincy *Adams*

Our Sixth President

By Gerry and Janet Souter

SPIRIT
of America™

The Child's World®, Inc.
Chanhassen, Minnesota

7

JOHN QUINCY *Adams*

Published in the United States of America by The Child's World®, Inc.
PO Box 326 • Chanhassen, MN 55317-0326 • 800-599-READ • www.childsworld.com

Acknowledgments
The Creative Spark: Mary Francis-DeMarois, Project Director; Elizabeth Sirimarco Budd, Series Editor; Robert Court, Design and Art Direction; Janine Graham, Page Layout; Jennifer Moyers, Production

The Child's World®, Inc.: Mary Berendes, Publishing Director; Red Line Editorial, Fact Research; Cindy Klingel, Curriculum Advisor; Robert Noyed, Historical Advisor

Photos
Cover: White House Collection, courtesy White House Historical Association; Courtesy Adams National Historical Park: 6, 7, 10, 12, 14, 15, 23, 24, 28, 29, 31; Bettmann/Corbis: 25, 27, 30, 34; Corbis: 20, 22; Kevin Davidson: 17; Gianni Dagli Orti/Corbis: 18; The Library of Congress Collection: 11; Courtesy of the Massachusetts Historical Society: 8; Museum of the City of New York/Corbis: 13; Stock Montage: 35

Library of Congress Cataloging-in-Publication Data
Souter, Gerry.
    John Quincy Adams / Gerry and Janet Souter.
        p. cm.
    Includes bibliographical references and index.
    ISBN 1-56766-846-1 (lib. bdg. : alk. paper)
    1. Adams, John Quincy, 1767–1848—Juvenile literature. 2. Presidents—United States—Biography—Juvenile literature. [1. Adams, John Quincy, 1767–1848. 2. Presidents.]
    I. Souter, Janet, 1940– II. Title.
    E377 .S7 2001
    973.5'5'092—dc21
                                                    00-011493

Contents

Chapter ONE

In His Father's Footsteps

John Quincy Adams was the sixth president of the United States. He was the son of the nation's second president, John Adams.

THE PATH IN LIFE THAT JOHN QUINCY ADAMS would follow took shape the moment his parents knew they had a son. He was born on July 11, 1767, on the family farm. The Adamses lived in the town of Braintree, Massachusetts. (Braintree was later renamed Quincy.) His father, John Adams, would soon help run the country during the American **Revolution.** Later he would become the second U.S. president. But when John Quincy was born, John Adams was a little-known country lawyer. America had not even declared its independence yet. Still, the family dreamed of achieving great things. Devoting one's life to **politics** became a family tradition.

In 1774, John Adams was elected to the **Continental Congress.** This meant he had

to leave Massachusetts for Philadelphia, where
the Congress met. John Quincy and his older
sister were left in their mother's care. But their
father gave careful instructions about how to
raise them. He wrote to his wife, Abigail, of
her duty to shape "the minds and manners
of our children." John Adams wanted his
children not only to be good, but to succeed
as well. To succeed, he said, Abigail had to
teach them to work hard and keep busy.

*John Quincy Adams was
born on his family's farm
in the house at left. His
father was born in the
house next door.*

John and Abigail Adams (above) hoped their first-born son would follow in his father's footsteps. John Adams was devoted to his country and was elected to its most important office. Abigail wanted John Quincy to achieve the same thing. She once wrote to him, "If you do not rise to the head of your country, it will be owing to your own laziness."

Six-year-old John Quincy thought about this advice. He wrote a letter to his father, saying he had spent too much time playing and having fun. "There is a great deal of room for me to grow better," he said. Throughout his life, John Quincy would always feel he could do better. He would always worry that he was not working hard enough.

On April 19, 1775, the American Revolution began. That June, John Quincy held his mother's hand and climbed nearby

Penn Hill. They could see the smoke of gunpowder drift across Bunker Hill, where a battle was taking place. They listened to the sounds of cannons being fired as British and American soldiers faced each other in combat. Watching the event unfold so close to home frightened John Quincy, but it also excited him. He began to understand the American quest for freedom.

In 1778, John Quincy's father was sent to France. His **mission** was to ask the French king for help. The Revolution was expensive and difficult. Americans needed more soldiers and supplies. John Adams brought his bright 10-year-old son with him to act as his secretary—John Quincy's first job in politics. He was enrolled at school and began to study the French language. In a letter to his wife, John Adams bragged that their son "learned more French in one day than I could learn in a week."

John and John Quincy soon returned to the United States and were very happy to see their family again. But almost as soon as they arrived, the Continental Congress had a new job for John Adams. In 1780, he was on his way back to France. This time, both John

Quincy and his younger brother, Charles, went with their father.

John Quincy again worked as his father's secretary. At age 14, he traveled to St. Petersburg, Russia. He went there to work for a U.S. **diplomat.** At that time, foreign diplomats usually talked to each other in French. The diplomat asked John Quincy to come with him because the young boy spoke French perfectly. He would be the diplomat's **translator.**

A year later, John Quincy toured much of Europe. He ended up in Holland's capital, where his father was working. The United States had just signed a peace **treaty** with England after eight long years of war. The country needed money to set up its new government and to pay debts from the war. John Adams's task was to get a loan from Holland for the United States. John Quincy again worked as his father's secretary until it was time for them to go home. By that time, he had been in Europe for several years.

While in Holland with his father, John Quincy enjoyed horseback riding and ice-skating. But he spent most of his time studying and working hard to make his parents proud of him.

Once back in Massachusetts, John Quincy entered Harvard, which was the finest college in the country. He studied there for two years before graduating in 1787.

John Quincy hoped to become a lawyer, just as his father had been. He moved to Connecticut to work for a lawyer while he studied law. In 1789, his father became the vice president of the United States. One year later, John Quincy Adams opened his first law office.

John Quincy attended Harvard College, just like his father had years before. Other students at Harvard remarked that John Quincy was "stiff and formal." His travels through Europe had made him different from his American peers. Even John Quincy described himself as cold and silent.

▶ Braintree, the birthplace of John and John Quincy Adams, was renamed Quincy in 1792 in honor of Colonel John Quincy. He was the first member of the Adams family to live there. The name is pronounced "Kwin-zee" (not "Kwin-see"), just as Colonel Quincy pronounced his last name.

While working as a lawyer, John Quincy found time to write newspaper articles about the government. President Washington read many of these. He recognized the young writer's talent with words. He knew that John Quincy had spent much of his life in foreign countries and spoke many languages. President Washington believed he could help the country. He **appointed** John Quincy **minister** to Holland.

At the age of 26, John Quincy Adams was well on his way to a successful career. His family was proud and hopeful, certain that he would become an important American leader, just like his father. "All my hopes are in him," wrote John Adams of his son, "both for my family and country." All his life, John Quincy would strive to please his family. But he would always worry that he wasn't living up to their **expectations.**

President George Washington recognized that John Quincy Adams would be an excellent diplomat.

IN 1778, JOHN Adams was sent to France on a special mission. His task was to convince the French king to help America win the Revolution. Adams decided to take 10-year-old John Quincy with him.

On the night of February 13, Adams bundled his young son in a blanket, and they boarded the *Boston*. This ship would take them across the Atlantic, but they had no idea how difficult the crossing would be.

First, a squadron of British ships chased the *Boston* for two days after it left the harbor. Then icy cold winds tossed the ship to and fro. The wintry crossing of the Atlantic Ocean was terrifying, with high waves and blowing gales. At one point, a bolt of lightning struck the ship. It injured more than 20 sailors. Eventually, the *Boston* sailed free of the storm, only to discover a British ship sailing nearby. The captain wanted to attack the British craft, but it would be John Adams's decision. As young John Quincy watched the sails of the distant ship, his father ordered the attack.

John Quincy was sent below deck but watched the battle through an open porthole. Cannonballs whizzed across the deck of the *Boston,* just missing John Adams's head. Finally, the British ship surrendered.

Still later, an officer was hurt while firing a signal gun. Young John Quincy watched his father hold the officer's head while the ship's surgeon cut off the man's badly injured arm. By the time the *Boston* reached France, John Quincy Adams had received an education in war and survival.

Chapter TWO

A Career in Politics

John Quincy worked in Europe as a diplomat from 1796 until 1801. He was pleased when the U.S. government finally sent him home. He said he was never truly happy away from his parents and the family farm.

DURING HIS STAY IN HOLLAND, JOHN QUINCY Adams traveled to England. There he met Louisa Catherine Johnson, the daughter of a U.S. diplomat. She was charming and independent. She was also from a wealthy family. John Quincy knew that her wealth could help him in his career. He asked her to marry him, and she accepted. But shortly after, her father announced that he had lost all his money. John Quincy was disappointed, for the family money would have helped his career in politics. But he kept his promise and married Louisa in 1797.

By then, John Adams was the country's second president. He appointed his son the U.S. minister to Prussia, which was part of the kingdom of Germany. John Quincy and Louisa packed their bags and traveled to

14

Berlin, the capital city of Prussia. They stayed there until the spring of 1801. Then they set sail for the United States with their infant son, George.

Back in Massachusetts, John Quincy served briefly as a state senator. Then he was elected to the U.S. Senate in 1802. At the time, the two major **political parties** in the United States were the **Federalists** and the **Democratic-Republicans.** The Federalists controlled the Senate, and John Quincy's father was a Federalist. Thomas Jefferson led the Democratic-Republicans. The two parties often had bitter disagreements.

This painting of Louisa Catherine Johnson was painted about the time of her marriage to John Quincy Adams. The couple would have three sons and a daughter together, and the marriage would last 50 years until John Quincy's death in 1848.

The Federalists helped John Quincy get elected to the Senate. They hoped that he would support them. After all, his father was a Federalist, too. But John Quincy was an independent thinker. He followed his own beliefs and often opposed the Federalists. For one thing, he supported Jefferson's decision to purchase a huge piece of land from the French. The "Louisiana Purchase" more than doubled the size of the United States. Even so, the Federalists were furious that a member of their party would support anything proposed by Jefferson, the enemy of their party. John Quincy learned he could make enemies by thinking for himself.

John Quincy also sided with Jefferson on the **Embargo** Act of 1807. The English had been attacking U.S. ships at sea. Jefferson wanted this to stop. The Embargo Act stopped American ships from taking goods to England—or to anywhere else in Europe. European ships could not enter American ports either. Jefferson believed this might force England to leave American ships alone. He thought the British would lose money without American goods. Eventually, they

The map contains the following labels:

CLAIMED BY ENGLAND, RUSSIA, SPAIN, and UNITED STATES

SPANISH TERRITORIES

LOUISIANA PURCHASE

OLD NORTHWEST

MISSISSIPPI TERRITORY

MT, ND, WY, SD, MN, NE, IA, CO, KS, MO, NM, TX, OK, AR, LA, OH, KY, TN, VT, ME, NH, NY, MA, CT, RI, PA, NJ, MD, DC, DE, VA, NC, SC, GA

0 100 200 400 600 MILES

would want American goods badly enough and agree to stop attacking American ships.

The Federalists were against the embargo. It made them very angry when John Quincy supported Jefferson yet again. But he would not let the Federalists tell him what to do or how to think. The angry Federalists met in Boston in 1808. They decided to support a different **candidate** for the Senate in the next election. Adams felt it was impossible

Adams supported President Jefferson's Louisiana Purchase, even though his political party opposed everything Jefferson did. Adams believed it was a good decision. The purchase increased the size of the United States by more than 800,000 square miles.

President Madison named John Quincy Adams the minister to Russia in 1809. John Quincy, Louisa, and their youngest son set sail for the Russian capital of St. Petersburg, shown above. The two older boys stayed with their grandparents in Massachusetts. The family would not be together again until 1815.

to continue his work after such an insult, so he **resigned** from the Senate.

Adams spent a relaxing year reading and gardening in Massachusetts. But the nation's leaders had not forgotten him. In 1809, President James Madison appointed Adams the minister to Russia. He and his family soon left for St. Petersburg.

18

At home, the War of 1812 broke out against England. The British had been kidnapping American sailors at sea, claiming that they were **deserters** from the British navy. Russia and Great Britain were **allies.** John Quincy spent most of his time explaining to the Russians why the United States was at war with England. He was able to win the trust and respect of the Russian leaders. By 1814, the U.S. government asked Adams to travel to the city of Ghent in Belgium. There he would **negotiate** a peace treaty with Great Britain.

Adams and the British official spent much time "erasing, patching, and mending" the agreement between the two nations. Finally, the Treaty of Ghent was signed on Christmas Eve of 1814. The War of 1812 was over. President Madison named Adams the post-war minister to Great Britain, a position his father had held after the Revolution.

James Monroe was elected the fifth president in 1816. He appointed Adams as his **secretary of state.** Adams and his family returned to the United States, this time to stay.

Adams's experience as a diplomat helped to make him an excellent secretary of state.

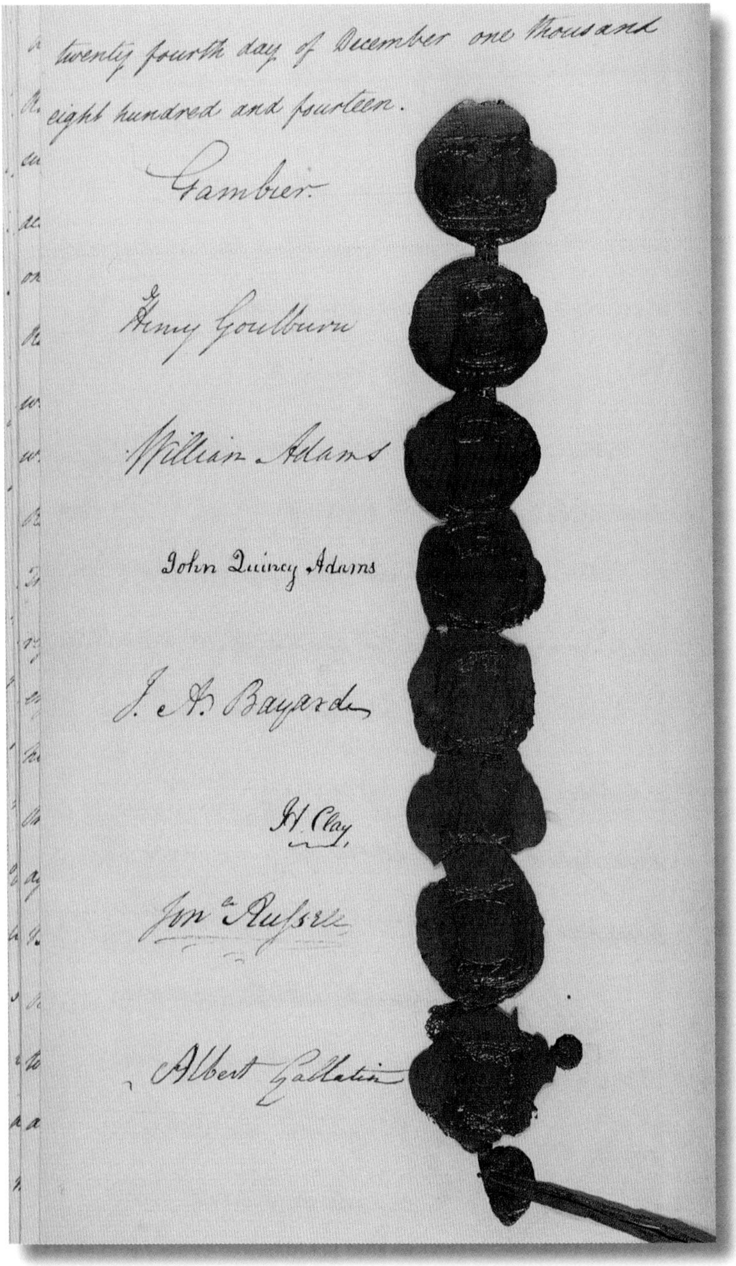

twenty fourth day of December one thousand
eight hundred and fourteen.

Gambier.

Henry Goulburn

William Adams

John Quincy Adams

J. A. Bayard

H Clay

Jon Russell

Albert Gallatin

In 1814, Adams negotiated the Treaty of Ghent, which ended the War of 1812. His signature, along with those of other leaders, is shown here on the official document.

The United States already controlled much of Florida, but Spain still possessed the eastern part of it. In 1819, Adams negotiated a treaty with Spain. The Spanish agreed to give up their land in Florida for $5 million. The following year, the **territory** of Missouri wanted to join the **Union.** Southern slave owners wanted Missouri to enter as a slave state. Adams was firmly against slavery. He convinced President Monroe to sign the Missouri Compromise of 1820. This admitted Missouri as a slave state only if Maine entered as a free state, where slavery was illegal.

During Monroe's second term as president, European countries were trying to control parts

of South and Central America. The United
States did not want Europe to gain power in
any part of the Americas. In 1823, Adams and
President Monroe wrote the Monroe **Doctrine.**
In this statement, the United States promised
to fight any European nation that attempted to
colonize any part of North, Central, or South
America. The doctrine is still in effect today.
It gives the United States the power to stop
attacks on its southern neighbors.

Although many people did not like the
outspoken Adams, he did have his supporters.
They encouraged him to run for president
in 1824. Adams knew that a war hero named
Andrew Jackson had the support of the
American people. Even so, he decided to run
for office. But he still refused to **campaign** for
people's votes. He wanted people to vote for
him because they believed he would be a good
president, not because he campaigned for the
job. He also believed he deserved the office
and that it should be given to him as a reward
for his years of service to the country.

When the votes were counted, Andrew
Jackson had won the popular vote, which
means that more citizens voted for him than

for his opponents. But no candidate had won a majority of **electoral votes.** When this happens, the House of Representatives must choose the next president. By only one vote, John Quincy Adams became the sixth president of the United States.

James Monroe (standing beside the globe) and Adams (seated at far left) wanted to keep Europeans out of the Americas. As they drafted the Monroe Doctrine, they promised freedom to nations throughout the Western Hemisphere.

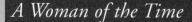

JOHN QUINCY ADAMS WAS A BRILLIANT man with an excellent education. He spoke French, Russian, and German and could read both Greek and Latin. But his wife, Louisa, was never given the opportunity to receive such an education. Women of the day were raised to be homemakers and hostesses. In a book of the time called *A Father's Legacy to His Daughter,* the author offered this advice to women: "If you happen to have any learning, keep it a profound secret, especially from the men."

Many girls from wealthy families were taught not how to read and write, but how to enter a room with grace, how to sit, and how to talk about acceptable topics. While John Quincy was pouring over his books, Louisa was learning proper table manners and a lady-like curtsy.

Fortunately, Louisa's parents saw the value in teaching their daughter music and literature. She learned to play the harp, and she loved to read. She also sang and wrote poetry. Louisa may not have had the same education her husband had, but she was determined to be more than just a pretty ornament at his parties. From 1818 until 1825, she campaigned to help her husband become the president. Although naturally shy, she visited the wives of congressmen, attended parties and balls, and gave numerous parties of her own. John Quincy was known to be cold and even rude, so Louisa's efforts were important. Her charm and personality won the couple many friends in Washington. Without her help, he might never have become president.

Chapter THREE

The Bitter Presidency

Although he won the presidency, John Quincy Adams failed to win the cooperation of Congress. This kept him from reaching his goals as president.

ON MARCH 4, 1825, JOHN QUINCY ADAMS gave a speech to the nation at his **inauguration.** He knew he had received only one-third of the popular vote and that many people wanted Andrew Jackson to be their president. Still, he promised he would work "with a heart devoted to the welfare of the country."

When John Quincy and Louisa moved into the president's mansion, it was a large and drafty home that Americans called the "White House." Their four years there would be difficult. John Quincy found it hard to achieve his goals. Although Andrew Jackson had not won the election, he still had many supporters in Congress. They often voted against Adams. He seemed to be nothing more than a **figurehead** until Andrew Jackson

Louisa Adams gave many parties as the first lady, including this one at which Andrew Jackson (center) was a guest. At such parties, Louisa always stayed close to John Quincy, helping him make polite conversation. She would steer him away when he began to get irritated with an opinion that did not match his own. Adams appreciated his wife's efforts and knew she was helpful to him. He once said, "I well know that I shall never be a popular man."

could win the presidency in the next election. But he was still determined to do his best.

Adams wanted the **federal** government to take an active role in helping the states. He proposed the "American System," which was a plan to make the nation **self-sufficient.** He wanted Americans to buy fewer goods from foreign countries and to rely on American-made items. To do this, his secretary of state, Henry Clay, suggested

Interesting Facts

▸ The most important national event during John Quincy Adams's presidency was the completion of the Erie Canal in 1825. This waterway traveled 363 miles across New York State from the Hudson River to Lake Erie. It made it much easier to transport goods from the Midwest to the East.

placing higher **tariffs** on foreign goods. Adams also wanted to begin building new roads and canals in the South and the West. These would make it easier to transport crops from these regions to the East Coast.

Congressmen blocked the American System. Some did so because they wanted to be sure that Andrew Jackson would win in the next election. Others believed that Adams's plans gave the federal government too much power. In the end, Congress would accept only two of his ideas. One plan improved roads in Ohio. The other was the construction of a new canal that connected the Ohio River and the Chesapeake Bay.

Adams also had little support from Congress in **foreign affairs.** His work on the Monroe Doctrine had created a friendship between the United States and Latin America. In his second year as president, Latin American leaders planned the Panama Congress. This event was organized to build friendly ties between American nations. It also set up a united force to fight against unfriendly countries. Mexico and Colombia asked the United States to send **representatives** to this meeting.

President Adams and Henry Clay believed that the United States should take part in the Panama Congress. After all, the U.S. was the most powerful nation in the Americas. They also wanted to promote friendship and trade between Latin America and the United States.

The U.S. Congress was against sending representatives to the meeting. Southern congressmen objected because the Latin American countries had outlawed slavery. Other leaders said it went against the U.S. policy of remaining **neutral.** U.S. representatives did not attend the Panama Congress.

Adams was the leader of the only remaining political party, the Democratic-Republicans. But people within the party disagreed with his ideas. Soon, the party broke into two groups.

Henry Clay also ran in the presidential election of 1824 but finished in last place. He was still a member of the House of Representatives and gave his support to Adams. This helped Adams win the presidency. He then appointed Clay as his secretary of state.

27

John Adams died on July 4, 1826, on the 50th anniversary of the signing of the Declaration of Independence. John Quincy was greatly saddened by his father's death.

Jackson's supporters called themselves the Democrats. Adams and his supporters called themselves the National Republicans.

To make a difficult time even worse, Adams learned in 1826 that his father was very ill. He rushed to Massachusetts to see him. Sadly, he arrived a week after his father had died. He said the death struck like "an arrow to my heart." John Quincy Adams felt sad and depressed.

The final two years of his presidency were very unhappy. As the next election grew closer, Jackson's forces began to tell lies about Adams. They called him a snob who hated the American people. They said he lived a life of luxury in the White House. To fight back, Adams's supporters claimed that Andrew Jackson was a murderer and a slave trader who was always ready for a fistfight. But few Americans seemed to care that Jackson was an uneducated military man and a southern slave owner. When the votes were counted, Jackson had won.

JOHN QUINCY ADAMS HAD TWO YOUNGER brothers, Thomas and Charles. They struggled with the high expectations of their parents. Thomas and Charles led sad, difficult lives. Only John Quincy was able to succeed in politics as his father had.

John Quincy Adams also had three sons, George, John, and Charles (shown from top to bottom). Like his father, John Quincy expected a great deal from his children. His oldest son, George, had problems with drinking and gambling. When John Quincy asked that they meet to discuss these problems, George grew frightened. He jumped over the side of a steamboat and drowned. John Quincy's second son, John, also drank heavily. He died from alcoholism in 1834, leaving only Charles to carry on the family name. "All my hopes in this world are now centered upon him," said John Quincy. Fortunately, Charles did find success in life. Like his father and grandfather, he had a brilliant career in politics. First, he was a congressman. Then during the American Civil War, he was appointed the minister to Great Britain.

Duty to the End

John Quincy Adams is shown here in an 1843 photograph. Years after he left office, Adams described his presidency as "the four most miserable years of my life."

JOHN QUINCY ADAMS LOST THE ELECTION OF 1828. He thought he had reached the end of his political career. "My own career is closed," he wrote in his diary, "The sun of my political life sets in the deepest gloom."

Once again, John Quincy returned to the family farm. And once again, the citizens of Massachusetts wanted him to take a seat in Congress. Some people wondered whether the former president should run for the House of Representatives. After all, he had held the most important position in the country. But when they asked Adams if he would consider it, he said, "No person should be **degraded** by serving the people as a Representative in Congress. Nor, in my opinion would a former President of the

United States be degraded by serving as a **selectman** of his town." When the votes were counted on November 6, 1830, he had won by a **landslide.** He would be reelected to the House for the next nine terms.

Adams was pleased to see that citizens still believed he was a good leader. "My election as President of the United States was not half as gratifying," he wrote in his diary the night of the election. "No election or appointment conferred upon me ever gave me so much pleasure." The people of Massachusetts still respected his intelligence and honesty.

After his presidency, Adams moved to the "Old House" on the family farm in Quincy. It was the home where his father had lived until his death in 1826.

At age 64, Adams entered the House of Representatives as a new congressman, representing about 50,000 people from Massachusetts. He earned a salary of $8 a day plus a travel allowance.

John Quincy Adams was called "Old Man **Eloquent**" by his fellow congressmen because he was such a good speaker. His most important goal was to fight slavery. He introduced many **petitions** to end it. Southern congressmen wanted to stop him. They created rules (called "gag rules") that kept any item opposing slavery from being read to Congress. They did what they could to silence Adams and others who were against it. But Adams would not give up. He continued to send the petitions to the House between 1836 and 1844 until Congress again opened discussions on the issue of slavery.

In 1841, Adams worked briefly as a lawyer to defend a group of African slaves. These men had taken over a slave ship called the *Amistad*. When the U.S. Navy captured the slaves, the government had to decide what to do with them. Adams used his skills as a lawyer to defend the men to the Supreme Court, the

Interesting Facts

▸ John Quincy Adams is the only former president to be elected to the House of Representatives.

▸ As an old man, Adams once said, "Old minds are like old horses; you must exercise them if you wish to keep them in working order."

most powerful court in the country. He won freedom for the former slaves, who finally returned to Africa.

It was not only for slaves that Adams fought. He also spoke out for the rights of Native Americans. He fought for freedom of speech. He encouraged scientific studies to increase knowledge. As a congressman for 17 straight years, John Quincy Adams became one of the most respected men in Washington, D.C.

Adams once swore he would die while serving his country. This promise came true. On February 21, 1848, the 80-year-old Adams gasped and slumped in his seat at the Capitol. He had suffered a **stroke.** He was carried to a nearby room where he would remain for the next two days. His doctors believed he was too ill to be moved, so the lifelong politician died at the U.S. Capitol.

For most of his life, John Quincy Adams had served his country. From his first role as secretary to his famous father to his 17 years in Congress, Adams devoted himself to politics. At his funeral, a senator said what many were thinking: "Where could death have found him, but at the post of duty?"

Interesting Facts

▶ During his terms in the House of Representatives, Adams was firmly against slavery. He once sent 350 petitions to the House in a single day. Many of these documents remained in the basement of the Capitol. In fact, a historian once discovered a janitor using them to light a fire in the Capitol's furnace.

▶ Shortly after John Quincy collapsed, Louisa Adams rushed to be by her husband's side. She had been told that he had only fainted, but arrived to find him in serious condition. She said it was a terrible shock "when I arrived there and found him speechless and dying, and without a moment of returning to show that he knew I was near him."

Adams tried to get up after he collapsed in the House chambers, but he fell back into his chair. He died at the Capitol building, serving his country to the end.

THE SPANISH SLAVE SHIP *AMISTAD* WAS CARRYING 53 SLAVES IN THE SUMMER OF 1839. They had been kidnapped from Africa, transported to the island of Cuba, and then sold to work at sugar plantations. They were on their way to a life of slavery when they were able to take control of the ship. The Africans killed the captain and the cook but kept two crew members alive to help sail the ship.

For two months, they sailed up the North American coastline. The journey was difficult. They were low on food and water. They also did not know how to sail the ship, and the two Spanish crew members would not help them. Finally, the U.S. Navy took control of the *Amistad* and captured the African men.

For two years, American **abolitionists** demanded that the men be freed and returned to Africa. At the same time, the Spanish government and the planters who had bought the slaves demanded that their "property" be returned. Finally, the case was sent to the Supreme Court, the most powerful court in the country. The abolitionists asked John Quincy Adams to defend the slaves. At first, he refused. He was older now and did not feel up to the challenge. Finally, he agreed, saying, "If, by the blessing of God, my health and strength shall permit, I will argue the case before the Supreme Court."

On the first day of his argument, he turned to the judges and pointed to a copy of the Declaration of Independence that hung across the room. He reminded those present that the Declaration states, "all men are created equal." He said that these words should count for the African men he was defending.

The Supreme Court took about one month to make a decision. The judges decided that the Africans had been illegally captured and must be set free. Abolitionists then raised money to help send the men home. The 35 surviving slaves arrived in Africa about three years after they were first captured.

1767 On July 11, John Quincy Adams is born on the Adams farm in Braintree (renamed Quincy in 1792), Massachusetts. He is the first son of John and Abigail Adams.

1775 The American Revolution begins on April 19, with the battles at Lexington and Concord in Massachusetts. That June, seven-year-old John Quincy climbs up Penn Hill to watch the Battle of Bunker Hill from a distance.

1778 The Continental Congress sends John Adams on a diplomatic mission to France. John Quincy goes with him and acts as his secretary.

1781 John Quincy, who now speaks perfect French, accompanies an American diplomat to Russia as a secretary and translator. (French was the language used by diplomats at the time.)

1782 John Quincy tours Europe.

1783 In April, John Quincy returns to Holland to serve as his father's secretary.

1785 John Quincy returns to the United States and attends Harvard for two years.

1790 John Quincy opens his first law office.

1794 President Washington appoints John Quincy Adams minister to Holland.

1796 John Adams is elected president.

1797 John Quincy marries Louisa Catherine Johnson on July 26. President John Adams appoints John Quincy Adams as minister to Prussia. Louisa and John Quincy set up housekeeping in Berlin.

1801 John Adams leaves the presidency. Thomas Jefferson becomes the third president. In the spring, John Quincy Adams and his family return to the United States.

1802 John Quincy Adams is elected to a six-year term as U.S. senator from Massachusetts. He is a member of the Federalist Party.

1808 During his time as senator, John Quincy Adams has angered the Federalists by siding too often with Thomas Jefferson, a Democratic-Republican. The Federalists meet in Boston and select a candidate to replace Adams in the next Senate election.

1809 President James Madison appoints John Quincy Adams minister to Russia. John Quincy and Louisa take their youngest son with them to live in St. Petersburg, the capital city of that country. The two older sons remain in Massachusetts with relatives.

1812 America goes to war against Britain.

1814 John Quincy Adams heads the American representatives who will forge a peace treaty with Great Britain. The treaty is signed on December 24, 1814.

1815 In January, before news of the Treaty of Ghent reaches the United States, Andrew Jackson and his soldiers defeat the British at the Battle of New Orleans.

1816 James Monroe is elected the fifth president. He appoints John Quincy Adams his secretary of state.

1817 John Quincy and his family sail for the United States.

1819 John Quincy negotiates the purchase of East Florida from Spain for $5 million.

1820 President Monroe signs the Missouri Compromise in 1820 at the urging of John Quincy Adams.

1823 The Monroe Doctrine is drafted by President Monroe with the help of John Quincy Adams.

1824 John Quincy Adams is urged to run for president. None of the four candidates wins a majority, so the House of Representatives must vote for the president.

1825 The House of Representatives elects John Quincy Adams as the sixth president on February 9. Andrew Jackson, who had been the people's choice for president, begins campaigning immediately for the next election. Adams's inauguration takes place on March 4. During the next four years, Adams will attempt to adopt the "American System," which will make the nation more self-sufficient. Unfortunately, many congressmen oppose Adams's plans.

1826 Adams attempts to send American representatives to the Panama Congress. This event was organized to build friendly ties among American nations. The U.S. Congress refuses to send any representatives to Panama. Adams's father, former president John Adams, dies on July 4, the 50th anniversary of the signing of the Declaration of Independence.

1828 Andrew Jackson is elected seventh president of the United States. John Quincy Adams retires, thinking his career in politics is finished.

1830 Friends convince Adams to run for Congress. At age 63, he is elected to the House of Representatives. He will be reelected eight times and spend the next 17 years as a congressman.

1831 Adams takes his seat at the House of Representatives. He begins his fight against slavery.

1836 Adams sends many petitions against slavery to be discussed in the House. Southern congressmen create "gag rules" to stop all petitions against slavery from being heard in Congress. Adams does not give up.

1841 John Quincy pleads the case for a group of African slaves who took over a Spanish slave ship, the *Amistad*. He wins, and the Africans are set free. Abolitionists eventually help them return to Africa.

1844 Thanks to Adams's efforts, the "gag rules" are overturned. Congress may again consider anti-slavery petitions.

1848 On February 21, John Quincy Adams is at the Capitol, preparing to vote, when he collapses from a stroke. He is taken to a quiet room where he dies two days later.

abolitionists (ab-uh-LISH-uh-nists)
Abolitionists were people who wanted to end slavery in the United States. Abolitionists fought to help the Africans who took over the Spanish slave ship *Amistad*.

allies (AL-lize)
Allies are nations that have agreed to help each other, for example, by fighting together against a common enemy. England and Russia were allies during the War of 1812.

appointed (uh-POYN-ted)
If someone is appointed to a position, he or she is asked by an important official to take a job. President Washington appointed John Quincy Adams the minister to Holland.

campaign (kam-PAYN)
A campaign is the process of running for an election, including activities such as giving speeches or attending rallies. John Quincy Adams refused to campaign for the presidency.

candidate (KAN-duh-det)
A candidate is a person running in an election. The Federalists selected a new candidate for senator when John Quincy Adams sided with the Democratic-Republicans.

Continental Congress (kon-tih-NEN-tul KONG-gris)
The Continental Congress was the group of men who governed the United States during and after the Revolution. John Adams was a member of the First Continental Congress.

degraded (dee-GRAY-ded)
If a person is degraded, he or she is dishonored or shamed. John Quincy Adams said a former president was not degraded by accepting a smaller position in the government.

Democratic-Republicans (dem-uh-KRAT-ik ree-PUB-luh-kenz)
The Democratic-Republicans were members of a political party. They believed that more citizens should be given the right to vote and take part in the federal government.

deserters (deh-ZER-turz)
Deserters are people who leave something that they shouldn't leave, such as the military. The British searched American ships for sailors they thought had deserted their navy.

Glossary Terms

diplomat (DIP-luh-mat)
A diplomat is a government official whose job is to represent a country in discussions with other countries. Both John Quincy Adams and his father were diplomats.

doctrine (DOK-trin)
A doctrine is something that a nation, religion, or other group firmly believes. John Quincy Adams helped President Monroe create the Monroe Doctrine.

**electoral votes
(ee-LEKT-uh-rul VOTZ)**
Electoral votes are those cast by representatives of the American public for the president and vice president. Each state chooses representatives who vote for a candidate in an election. These representatives vote according to what the majority of people in their state want.

eloquent (EL-oh-kwint)
If people are eloquent, they express themselves well. John Quincy Adams was known as "Old Man Eloquent" when he was in the House of Representatives.

embargo (em-BAR-goh)
An embargo stops one country from selling its goods to another country. The United States began an embargo against England in 1807.

expectations (ek-spek-TAY-shunz)
If people have high expectations, they expect good things from someone or something. Abigail and John Adams had high expectations for their son.

federal (FED-ur-ul)
Federal means having to do with the central government of the United States, rather than a state or city government. John Quincy Adams wanted the federal government to help the states.

Federalists (FED-ur-il-ists)
The Federalists were members of a political party in John Quincy Adams's time. Federalists believed that a few well-educated people should run the nation and that the central government should control the states.

figurehead (FIG-yer-hed)
A figurehead is a leader who has no real power. John Quincy Adams felt like a figurehead because Congress would not cooperate with him.

foreign affairs (FOR-un uh-FAIRZ)
Foreign affairs are matters involving other (foreign) countries. John Quincy Adams had trouble with both foreign affairs and issues in the United States.

39

**inauguration
(ih-naw-gyuh-RAY-shun)**
An inauguration is the ceremony that takes place when a new president begins a term. John Quincy Adams's inauguration took place on March 4, 1825.

landslide (LAND-slyd)
If a candidate wins an election by a landslide, he or she wins by a huge number of votes. John Quincy Adams won his election to the House of Representatives by a landslide.

minister (MIN-eh-stir)
A minister is a person who is in charge of one part of the government. The U.S. minister to France takes care of the relationship between the United States and France.

mission (MISH-un)
A mission is when a person is sent someplace for a special purpose. The government sent John Adams on a mission to ask the French king for help during the American Revolution.

negotiate (nee-GOH-she-ayt)
If people negotiate, they talk things over and try to come to an agreement. John Quincy Adams went to Ghent to negotiate a treaty with Great Britain.

neutral (NOO-trul)
If people are neutral, they do not take sides. Some people thought the Panama Congress went against the U.S. policy of remaining neutral.

petitions (puh-TISH-unz)
Petitions are written requests or demands for something. Congressmen send petitions to be heard by other members of Congress.

**political parties
(puh-LIT-uh-kul PAR-teez)**
Political parties are groups of people who share similar ideas about how to run a government. The two major political parties in the early years of the nation were the Federalists and the Democratic-Republicans.

politics (PAWL-uh-tiks)
Politics refers to the actions and practices of the government. John Quincy Adams and his father were both active in politics.

**representatives
(rep-ree-ZEN-tuh-tivs)**
Representatives are people who attend a meeting, having agreed to speak or act for others. The United States did not send send representatives to the Panama Congress.

resign (ree-ZYN)
If people resign, they give up a job or position. John Quincy Adams resigned from the Senate when the Federalists supported another candidate.

revolution (rev-uh-LOO-shun)
A revolution is something that causes a complete change in government. The American Revolution was a war fought between the United States and Great Britain.

**secretary of state
(SEK-ruh-tair-ee OF STAYT)**
The secretary of state is a close advisor to the president. He or she is involved with the nation's relations with other countries.

selectman (seh-LEKT-man)
A selectman is a person elected to a town's government. John Quincy Adams said it was not a disgrace for a former president to serve as a selectman.

self-sufficient (SELF-suh-FISH-ent)
If people are self-sufficient, they do not need help from others. John Quincy Adams wanted the United States to be self-sufficient.

stroke (STROHK)
A stroke is a sudden injury to the brain when a blood vessel breaks or becomes blocked. John Quincy Adams died from a stroke.

tariffs (TAIR-ifs)
Tariffs are taxes on goods that are brought in from another country. Secretary of State Clay suggested raising tariffs on foreign goods.

territory (TAIR-ih-tor-ee)
A territory is a land or region, especially land that belongs to a government. The territory of Missouri joined the Union as a slave state.

translator (TRANS-lay-ter)
A translator changes words from one language to another. John Quincy Adams translated French into English for an American diplomat.

treaty (TREE-tee)
A treaty is a formal agreement between nations. The United States signed a peace treaty with England after the Revolution.

union (YOON-yen)
A union is the joining together of two people or groups of people, such as states. The Union is another name for the United States.

Our PRESIDENTS

	President	Elected From	Life Span	Presidency	Political Party	First Lady
	George Washington	Virginia	1732–1799	1789–1797	None	Martha Dandridge Custis Washington
	John Adams	Massachusetts	1735–1826	1797–1801	Federalist	Abigail Smith Adams
	Thomas Jefferson	Virginia	1743–1826	1801–1809	Democratic-Republican	widower
	James Madison	Virginia	1751–1836	1809–1817	Democratic Republican	Dolley Payne Todd Madison
	James Monroe	Virginia	1758–1831	1817–1825	Democratic Republican	Elizabeth Kortright Monroe
	John Quincy Adams	Massachusetts	1767–1848	1825–1829	Democratic-Republican	Louisa Johnson Adams
	Andrew Jackson	Tennessee	1767–1845	1829–1837	Democrat	widower
	Martin Van Buren	New York	1782–1862	1837–1841	Democrat	widower
	William H. Harrison	Ohio	1773–1841	1841	Whig	Anna Symmes Harrison
	John Tyler	Virginia	1790–1862	1841–1845	Whig	Letitia Christian Tyler Julia Gardiner Tyler
	James K. Polk	Tennessee	1795–1849	1845–1849	Democrat	Sarah Childress Polk

Our PRESIDENTS

President	Elected From	Life Span	Presidency	Political Party	First Lady
Zachary Taylor	Virginia	1784–1850	1849–1850	Whig	Margaret Mackall Smith Taylor
Millard Fillmore	New York	1800–1874	1850–1853	Whig	Abigail Powers Fillmore
Franklin Pierce	New Hampshire	1804–1869	1853–1857	Democrat	Jane Means Appleton Pierce
James Buchanan	Pennsylvania	1791–1868	1857–1861	Democrat	never married
Abraham Lincoln	Kentucky	1809–1865	1861–1865	Republican	Mary Todd Lincoln
Andrew Johnson	North Carolina	1808–1875	1865–1869	Democrat	Eliza McCardle Johnson
Ulysses S. Grant	Ohio	1822–1885	1869–1877	Republican	Julia Dent Grant
Rutherford B. Hayes	Ohio	1822–1893	1877–1881	Republican	Lucy Webb Hayes
James A. Garfield	Ohio	1831–1881	1881	Republican	Lucretia Rudolph Garfield
Chester A. Arthur	Vermont	1829–1886	1881–1885	Republican	widower
Grover Cleveland	New Jersey	1837–1908	1885–1889	Democrat	Frances Folsom Cleveland

Our PRESIDENTS

President	Elected From	Life Span	Presidency	Political Party	First Lady
Benjamin Harrison	Ohio	1833–1901	1889–1893	Republican	Caroline Scott Harrison
Grover Cleveland	New Jersey	1837–1908	1893–1897	Democrat	Frances Folsom Cleveland
William McKinley	Ohio	1843–1901	1897–1901	Republican	Ida Saxton McKinley
Theodore Roosevelt	New York	1858–1919	1901–1909	Republican	Edith Kermit Carow Roosevelt
William H. Taft	Ohio	1857–1930	1909–1913	Republican	Helen Herron Taft
Woodrow Wilson	Virginia	1856–1924	1913–1921	Democrat	Ellen L. Axson Wilson Edith Bolling Galt Wilson
Warren G. Harding	Ohio	1865–1923	1921–1923	Republican	Florence Kling De Wolfe Harding
Calvin Coolidge	Vermont	1872–1933	1923–1929	Republican	Grace Goodhue Coolidge
Herbert C. Hoover	Iowa	1874–1964	1929–1933	Republican	Lou Henry Hoover
Franklin D. Roosevelt	New York	1882–1945	1933–1945	Democrat	Anna Eleanor Roosevelt Roosevelt
Harry S. Truman	Missouri	1884–1972	1945–1953	Democrat	Elizabeth Wallace Truman

Our PRESIDENTS

President	Elected From	Life Span	Presidency	Political Party	First Lady
Dwight D. Eisenhower	Texas	1890–1969	1953–1961	Republican	Mary "Mamie" Doud Eisenhower
John F. Kennedy	Massachusetts	1917–1963	1961–1963	Democrat	Jacqueline Bouvier Kennedy
Lyndon B. Johnson	Texas	1908–1973	1963–1969	Democrat	Claudia Alta Taylor Johnson
Richard M. Nixon	California	1913–1994	1969–1974	Republican	Thelma Catherine Ryan Nixon
Gerald Ford	Nebraska	1913–	1974–1977	Republican	Elizabeth "Betty" Bloomer Warren Ford
James Carter	Georgia	1924–	1977–1981	Democrat	Rosalynn Smith Carter
Ronald Reagan	Illinois	1911–	1981–1989	Republican	Nancy Davis Reagan
George Bush	Massachusetts	1924–	1989–1993	Republican	Barbara Pierce Bush
William Clinton	Arkansas	1946–	1993–2001	Democrat	Hillary Rodham Clinton
George W. Bush	Texas	1946–	2001–	Republican	Laura Welch Bush

Qualifications

To run for president, a candidate must

- be at least 35 years old
- be a citizen who was born in the United States
- have lived in the United States for 14 years

Term of Office

A president's term of office is four years. No president can stay in office for more than two terms.

Election Date

The presidential election takes place every four years on the first Tuesday of November.

Inauguration Date

Presidents are inaugurated on January 20.

Oath of Office

I do solemnly swear I will faithfully execute the office of the President of the United States and will to the best of my ability preserve, protect, and defend the Constitution of the United States.

Write a Letter to the President

One of the best things about being a U.S. citizen is that Americans get to participate in their government. They can speak out if they feel government leaders aren't doing their jobs. They can also praise leaders who are going the extra mile. Do you have something you'd like the president to do? Should the president worry more about the environment and encourage people to recycle? Should the government spend more money on our schools? You can write a letter to the president to say how you feel!

1600 Pennsylvania Avenue
Washington, D.C. 20500

You can even send an e-mail to: president@whitehouse.gov

For Further INFORMATION

Internet Sites

Find links to information about John Quincy Adams:
http://www.homeworkcentral.com/knowledge/vsl_sections.asp?sectionid=5388&tg=
HIST&flt=KE

Read quotations from John Quincy Adams:
http://www.bemorecreative.com/one/816.htm

Read John Quincy Adams's inaugural address:
http://gi.grolier.com/presidents/aae/inaugs/1825adam.html

Learn more about the War of 1812:
http://www.geocities.com/Heartland/Ranch/9198/war1812/w1812a.htm

Learn more about Adams's secretary of state, Henry Clay:
http://www.bellenet.com/clay.html

Learn more about Louisa Catherine Adams:
http://www.whitehouse.gov/WH/glimpse/firstladies/html/la6.html

Take a quick tour of Quincy, Massachusetts:
http://www.key-biz.com/ssn/Quincy/tour.html

Learn more about the *Amistad* and slavery:
http://amistad.mysticseaport.org/main/welcome.html

Learn more about all the presidents and visit the White House:
http://www.whitehouse.gov/WH/glimpse/presidents/html/presidents.html
http://www.thepresidency.org/presinfo.htm
http://www.americanpresidents.org/

Books

Chambers, Veronica. *Amistad Rising: A Story of Freedom.* Austin, TX: Raintree/
Steck-Vaughn, 1998.

Collier, Christopher, and James Lincoln. *Andrew Jackson's America.* New York:
Marshall Cavendish, 1999.

Gormley, Beatrice. *First Ladies: Women Who Called the White House Home.*
New York: Scholastic Trade, 1997.

Walker, Jane C. *John Quincy Adams* (United States Presidents). Springfield,
New Jersey: Enslow Publishers, 2000.

Index

333700000000007